Henry Wadsworth Longfellow, John Gilbert, Birket Foster,
John Absolon

Household Poems

Henry Wadsworth Longfellow, John Gilbert, Birket Foster, John Absolon

Household Poems

ISBN/EAN: 9783744796835

Printed in Europe, USA, Canada, Australia, Japan

Cover: Foto ©Thomas Meinert / pixelio.de

More available books at **www.hansebooks.com**

BY

HENRY W. LONGFELLOW.

With Illustrations by

JOHN GILBERT, BIRKET FOSTER, AND JOHN ABSOLON.

BOSTON:
TICKNOR AND FIELDS.
1865.

Entered according to Act of Congress, in the year 1865, by

HENRY W. LONGFELLOW,

in the Clerk's Office of the District Court of the District of Massachusetts.

[NOTE. — These selections from the poems of MR. LONGFELLOW are made by the Publishers to supply a demand for all his shorter pieces of a domestic character in a single inexpensive volume of a portable shape.]

UNIVERSITY PRESS:
WELCH, BIGELOW, AND COMPANY,
CAMBRIDGE.

CONTENTS.

DEDICATION.

As one who, walking in the twilight gloom,
  Hears round about him voices as it darkens,
And seeing not the forms from which they come,
  Pauses from time to time, and turns and hearkens,

So walking here in twilight, O my friends!
  I hear your voices, softened by the distance,
And pause, and turn to listen, as each sends
  His words of friendship, comfort, and assistance.

If any thought of mine, or sung or told,
  Has ever given delight or consolation,
Ye have repaid me back a thousand fold,
  By every friendly sign and salutation.

Thanks for the sympathies that ye have shown!
  Thanks for each kindly word, each silent token,
That teaches me, when seeming most alone,
  Friends are around us, though no word be spoken.

Kind messages, that pass from land to land;
  Kind letters, that betray the heart's deep history,
In which we feel the pressure of a hand, —
  One touch of fire, — and all the rest is mystery!

The pleasant books, that silently among
  Our household treasures take familiar places,
And are to us as if a living tongue
  Spake from the printed leaves or pictured faces!

Perhaps on earth I never shall behold,
  With eye of sense, your outward form and semblance;
Therefore to me ye never will grow old,
  But live forever young in my remembrance.

Never grow old, nor change, nor pass away!
  Your gentle voices will flow on forever,
When life grows bare and tarnished with decay,
  As through a leafless landscape flows a river.

Not chance of birth or place has made us friends,
  Being oftentimes of different tongues and nations,
But the endeavor for the selfsame ends,
  With the same hopes, and fears, and aspirations.

Therefore I hope to join your seaside walk,
  Saddened, and mostly silent, with emotion;
Not interrupting with intrusive talk
  The grand, majestic symphonies of ocean.

Therefore I hope, as no unwelcome guest,
  At your warm fireside, when the lamps are lighted,
To have my place reserved among the rest,
  Nor stand as one unsought and uninvited!

HOUSEHOLD POEMS.

HYMN TO THE NIGHT.

'Ασπασίη, τρίλλιστος.

I HEARD the trailing garments of the Night
   Sweep through her marble halls!
I saw her sable skirts all fringed with light
   From the celestial walls!

I felt her presence, by its spell of might,
   Stoop o'er me from above;
The calm, majestic presence of the Night,
   As of·the one I love.

I heard the sounds of sorrow and delight,
   The manifold, soft chimes,
That fill the haunted chambers of the Night,
   Like some old poet's rhymes.

From the cool cisterns of the midnight air
   My spirit drank repose;
The fountain of perpetual peace flows there, —
   From those deep cisterns flows.

O holy Night! from thee I learn to bear
   What man has borne before!
Thou layest thy finger on the lips of Care,
   And they complain no more.

Peace! Peace! Orestes-like I breathe this prayer!
Descend with broad-winged flight,
The welcome, the thrice-prayed for, the most fair,
The best-beloved Night!

A PSALM OF LIFE.

WHAT THE HEART OF THE YOUNG MAN SAID TO THE PSALMIST.

TELL me not, in mournful numbers,
   "Life is but an empty dream!"
For the soul is dead that slumbers,
   And things are not what they seem.

Life is real! Life is earnest!
   And the grave is not its goal;
"Dust thou art, to dust returnest,"
   Was not spoken of the soul.

Not enjoyment, and not sorrow,
   Is our destined end or way;
But to act, that each to-morrow
   Find us farther than to-day.

Art is long, and Time is fleeting,
   And our hearts, though stout and brave,
Still, like muffled drums, are beating
   Funeral marches to the grave.

In the world's broad field of battle,
   In the bivouac of Life,
Be not like dumb, driven cattle!
   Be a hero in the strife!

Trust no Future, howe'er pleasant!
   Let the dead Past bury its dead!
Act,—act in the living Present!
   Heart within, and God o'erhead!

THE REAPER AND THE FLOWERS.

Lives of great men all remind us
    We can make our lives sublime,
And, departing, leave behind us
    Footprints on the sands of time ;

Footprints, that perhaps another,
    Sailing o'er life's solemn main,
A forlorn and shipwrecked brother,
    Seeing, shall take heart again.

Let us, then, be up and doing,
    With a heart for any fate ;
Still achieving, still pursuing,
    Learn to labor and to wait.

THE REAPER AND THE FLOWERS.

THERE is a Reaper, whose name is Death,
    And, with his sickle keen,
He reaps the bearded grain at a breath,
    And the flowers that grow between.

"Shall I have nought that is fair ? " saith he ;
    " Have nought but the bearded grain ?
Though the breath of these flowers is sweet to me,
    I will give them all back again."

He gazed at the flowers with tearful eyes,
    He kissed their drooping leaves ;
It was for the Lord of Paradise
    He bound them in his sheaves.

" My Lord has need of these flowerets gay,"
    The Reaper said, and smiled ;
" Dear tokens of the earth are they,
    Where he was once a child.
    1 *

"They shall all bloom in fields of light,
  Transplanted by my care,
And saints, upon their garments white,
  These sacred blossoms wear."

And the mother gave, in tears and pain,
  The flowers she most did love;
She knew she should find them all again
  In the fields of light above.

O, not in cruelty, not in wrath,
  The Reaper came that day;
'T was an angel visited the green earth,
  And took the flowers away.

THE LIGHT OF STARS.

THE night is come, but not too soon;
  And sinking silently,
All silently, the little moon
  Drops down behind the sky.

There is no light in earth or heaven,
  But the cold light of stars;
And the first watch of night is given
  To the red planet Mars.

Is it the tender star of love?
  The star of love and dreams?
O no! from that blue tent above,
  A hero's armor gleams.

And earnest thoughts within me rise,
  When I behold afar,
Suspended in the evening skies,
  The shield of that red star.

O star of strength! I see thee stand
  And smile upon my pain;
Thou beckonest with thy mailed hand,
  And I am strong again.

Within my breast there is no light,
  But the cold light of stars;
I give the first watch of the night
  To the red planet Mars.

The star of the unconquered will,
  He rises in my breast,
Serene, and resolute, and still,
  And calm, and self-possessed;

And thou, too, whosoe'er thou art,
   That readest this brief psalm,
As one by one thy hopes depart,
   Be resolute and calm.

O fear not in a world like this,
   And thou shalt know erelong,
Know how sublime a thing it is
   To suffer and be strong.

FOOTSTEPS OF ANGELS.

WHEN the hours of Day are numbered,
   And the voices of the Night
Wake the better soul, that slumbered,
   To a holy, calm delight;

Ere the evening lamps are lighted,
   And, like phantoms grim and tall,
Shadows from the fitful fire-light
   Dance upon the parlor wall;

Then the forms of the departed
   Enter at the open door;
The beloved, the true-hearted,
   Come to visit me once more;

He, the young and strong, who cherished
   Noble longings for the strife,
By the roadside fell and perished,
   Weary with the march of life!

They, the holy ones and weakly,
   Who the cross of suffering bore,
Folded their pale hands so meekly,
   Spake with us on earth no more!

And with them the Being Beauteous,
   Who unto my youth was given,

More than all things else to love me,
  And is now a saint in heaven.

With a slow and noiseless footstep
  Comes that messenger divine,
Takes the vacant chair beside me,
  Lays her gentle hand in mine.

And she sits and gazes at me
  With those deep and tender eyes,
Like the stars, so still and saint-like,
  Looking downward from the skies.

Uttered not, yet comprehended,
  Is the spirit's voiceless prayer,
Soft rebukes, in blessings ended,
  Breathing from her lips of air.

O, though oft depressed and lonely,
  All my fears are laid aside,
If I but remember only
  Such as these have lived and died!

FLOWERS.

SPAKE full well, in language quaint and olden,
  One who dwelleth by the castled Rhine,
When he called the flowers, so blue and golden,
  Stars, that in earth's firmament do shine.

Stars they are, wherein we read our history,
  As astrologers and seers of eld;
Yet not wrapped about with awful mystery,
  Like the burning stars, which they beheld.

Wondrous truths, and manifold as wondrous,
  God hath written in those stars above;
But not less in the bright flowerets under us
  Stands the revelation of his love.

Bright and glorious is that revelation,
  Written all over this great world of ours;
Making evident our own creation,
  In these stars of earth, — these golden flowers.

And the Poet, faithful and far-seeing,
  Sees, alike in stars and flowers, a part
Of the self-same, universal being,
  Which is throbbing in his brain and heart.

Gorgeous flowerets in the sunlight shining,
  Blossoms flaunting in the eye of day,
Tremulous leaves, with soft and silver lining,
  Buds that open only to decay;

Brilliant hopes, all woven in gorgeous tissues,
  Flaunting gayly in the golden light;
Large desires, with most uncertain issues,
  Tender wishes, blossoming at night!

These in flowers and men are more than seeming,
  Workings are they of the self-same powers, ·
Which the Poet, in no idle dreaming,
  Seeth in himself and in the flowers.

Everywhere about us are they glowing,
  Some like stars, to tell us Spring is born;
Others, their blue eyes with tears o'erflowing,
  Stand like Ruth amid the golden corn;

Not alone in Spring's armorial bearing,
  And in Summer's green-emblazoned field,
But in arms of brave old Autumn's wearing,
  In the centre of his brazen shield;

Not alone in meadows and green alleys,
  On the mountain-top, and by the brink
Of sequestered pools in woodland valleys,
  Where the slaves of Nature stoop to drink;

Not alone in her vast dome of glory,
  Not on graves of bird and beast alone,
But in old cathedrals, high and hoary,
  On the tombs of heroes, carved in stone ;

In the cottage of the rudest peasant,
  In ancestral homes, whose crumbling towers,
Speaking of the Past unto the Present,
  Tell us of the ancient Games of Flowers ;

In all places, then, and in all seasons,
  Flowers expand their light and soul-like wings,
Teaching us, by most persuasive reasons,
  How akin they are to human things.

And with childlike, credulous affection
  We behold their tender buds expand ;
Emblems of our own great resurrection,
  Emblems of the bright and better land.

THE BELEAGUERED CITY.

I HAVE read, in some old marvellous tale,
  Some legend strange and vague,
That a midnight host of spectres pale
  Beleaguered the walls of Prague.

Beside the Moldau's rushing stream,
  With the wan moon overhead,
There stood, as in an awful dream,
  The army of the dead.

White as a sea-fog, landward bound,
  The spectral camp was seen,
And, with a sorrowful, deep sound,
  The river flowed between.

No other voice nor sound was there,
  No drum, nor sentry's pace;
The mistlike banners clasped the air,
  As clouds with clouds embrace.

But, when the old cathedral bell
  Proclaimed the morning prayer,
The white pavilions rose and fell
  On the alarmed air.

Down the broad valley fast and far
  The troubled army fled;
Up rose the glorious morning star,
  The ghastly host was dead.

I have read, in the marvellous heart of man,
  That strange and mystic scroll,
That an army of phantoms vast and wan
  Beleaguer the human soul.

Encamped beside Life's rushing stream,
  In Fancy's misty light,
Gigantic shapes and shadows gleam
  Portentous through the night.

Upon its midnight battle-ground
  The spectral camp is seen,
And, with a sorrowful, deep sound,
  Flows the River of Life between.

No other voice, nor sound is there,
  In the army of the grave;
No other challenge breaks the air,
  But the rushing of Life's wave.

And, when the solemn and deep church-bell
  Entreats the soul to pray,
The midnight phantoms feel the spell,
  The shadows sweep away.

Down the broad Vale of Tears afar
  The spectral camp is fled;
Faith shineth as a morning star,
  Our ghastly fears are dead.

MIDNIGHT MASS FOR THE DYING YEAR.

YES, the Year is growing old,
  And his eye is pale and bleared!
Death, with frosty hand and cold,
  Plucks the old man by the beard,
      Sorely, — sorely!

The leaves are falling, falling,
  Solemnly and slow;
Caw! caw! the rooks are calling,
  It is a sound of woe,
      A sound of woe!

Through woods and mountain passes
  The winds, like anthems, roll;
They are chanting solemn masses,
  Singing; "Pray for this poor soul,
    Pray, — pray!"

And the hooded clouds, like friars,
  Tell their beads in drops of rain,
And patter their doleful prayers! —
  But their prayers are all in vain,
    All in vain!

Thère he stands in the foul weather,
  The foolish, fond Old Year,
Crowned with wild flowers and with heather,
  Like weak, despised Lear,
    A king, — a king!

Then comes the summer-like day,
  Bids the old man rejoice!
His joy! his last! O, the old man gray,
  Loveth that ever-soft voice,
    Gentle and low.

To the crimson woods he saith, —
  To the voice gentle and low
Of the soft air, like a daughter's breath, —
  "Pray do not mock me so!
    Do not laugh at me!"

And now the sweet day is dead;
  Cold in his arms it lies;
No stain from its breath is spread
  Over the glassy skies,
    No mist or stain!

Then, too, the Old Year dieth,
  And the forests utter a moan,
Like the voice of one who crieth
  In the wilderness alone,
    "Vex not his ghost!"

Then comes, with an awful roar,
    Gathering and sounding on,
The storm-wind from Labrador,
    The wind Euroclydon,
      The storm-wind!

Howl! howl! and from the forest
    Sweep the red leaves away!
Would, the sins that thou abhorrest,
    O Soul! could thus decay,
      And be swept away!

For there shall come a mightier blast,
    There shall be a darker day;
And the stars, from heaven down-cast,
    Like red leaves be swept away!
      Kyrie, eleyson!
      Christe, eleyson!

THE RAINY DAY.

THE day is cold, and dark, and dreary;
　It rains, and the wind is never weary;
The vine still clings to the mouldering wall,
But at every gust the dead leaves fall,
　　And the day is dark and dreary.

My life is cold, and dark, and dreary;
It rains, and the wind is never weary;
My thoughts still cling to the mouldering Past,
But the hopes of youth fall thick in the blast,
　　And the days are dark and dreary.

Be still, sad heart! and cease repining;
Behind the clouds is the sun still shining;
Thy fate is the common fate of all,
Into each life some rain must fall,
　　Some days must be dark and dreary.

IT IS NOT ALWAYS MAY.

NO HAY PÁJAROS EN LOS NIDOS DE ANTAÑO.
　　　　　　　　　Spanish Proverb.

THE sun is bright, — the air is clear,
　The darting swallows soar and sing,
And from the stately elms I hear
　The blue-bird prophesying Spring.

So blue yon winding river flows,
　It seems an outlet from the sky,
Where waiting till the west wind blows,
　The freighted clouds at anchor lie.

All things are new; — the buds, the leaves,
　That gild the elm-tree's nodding crest,
And even the nest beneath the eaves; —
　There are no birds in last year's nest!

All things rejoice in youth and love,
　The fulness of their first delight!
And learn from the soft heavens above
　The melting tenderness of night.

Maiden, that read'st this simple rhyme,
　Enjoy thy youth, it will not stay;
Enjoy the fragrance of thy prime,
　For O! it is not always May!

Enjoy the Spring of Love and Youth,
　To some good angel leave the rest;
For Time will teach thee soon the truth,
　There are no birds in last year's nest!

THE VILLAGE BLACKSMITH.

UNDER a spreading chestnut-tree
　The village smithy stands;
The smith, a mighty man is he,
　With large and sinewy hands;
And the muscles of his brawny arms
　Are strong as iron bands.

His hair is crisp, and black, and long,
　His face is like the tan;
His brow is wet with honest sweat,
　He earns whate'er he can,
And looks the whole world in the face,
　For he owes not any man.

Week in, week out, from morn till night,
  You can hear his bellows blow;
You can hear him swing his heavy sledge,
  With measured beat and slow,
Like a sexton ringing the village bell,
  When the evening sun is low.

And children coming home from school
  Look in at the open door;
They love to see the flaming forge,
  And hear the bellows roar,
And catch the burning sparks that fly
  Like chaff from a threshing floor.

He goes on Sunday to the church,
  And sits among his boys;
He hears the parson pray and preach,
  He hears his daughter's voice,
Singing in the village choir,
  And it makes his heart rejoice.

It sounds to him like her mother's voice,
  Singing in Paradise!
He needs must think of her once more,
  How in the grave she lies;
And with his hard, rough hand he wipes
  A tear out of his eyes.

Toiling, — rejoicing, — sorrowing,
　Onward through life he goes;
Each morning sees some task begin,
　Each evening sees it close;
Something attempted, something done,
　Has earned a night's repose.

Thanks, thanks to thee, my worthy friend,
　For the lesson thou hast taught!
Thus at the flaming forge of life
　Our fortunes must be wrought;
Thus on its sounding anvil shaped
　Each burning deed and thought!

GOD'S-ACRE.

I LIKE that ancient Saxon phrase, which calls
　The burial-ground God's-Acre! It is just;
It consecrates each grave within its walls,
　And breathes a benison o'er the sleeping dust.

God's-Acre! Yes, that blessed name imparts
　Comfort to those, who in the grave have sown
The seed, that they had garnered in their hearts,
　Their bread of life, alas! no more their own.

Into its furrows shall we all be cast,
　In the sure faith, that we shall rise again
At the great harvest, when the archangel's blast
　Shall winnow, like a fan, the chaff and grain.

Then shall the good stand in immortal bloom,
　In the fair gardens of that second birth;
And each bright blossom, mingle its perfume
　With that of flowers, which never bloomed on earth.

With thy rude ploughshare, Death, turn up the sod,
    And spread the furrow for the seed we sow;
This is the field and Acre of our God,
    This is the place where human harvests grow!

TO THE RIVER CHARLES.

RIVER! that in silence windest
    Through the meadows, bright and free,
Till at length thy rest thou findest
    In the bosom of the sea!

Four long years of mingled feeling,
    Half in rest, and half in strife,
I have seen thy waters stealing
    Onward, like the stream of life.

Thou hast taught me, Silent River!
    Many a lesson, deep and long;
Thou hast been a generous giver;
    I can give thee but a song.

Oft in sadness and in illness
    I have watched thy current glide,
Till the beauty of its stillness
    Overflowed me, like a tide.

And in better hours and brighter,
    When I saw thy waters gleam,
I have felt my heart beat lighter,
    And leap onward with thy stream.

Not for this alone I love thee,
    Nor because thy waves of blue
From celestial seas above thee
    Take their own celestial hue.

Where yon shadowy woodlands hide thee,
 And thy waters disappear,
Friends I love have dwelt beside thee,
 And have made thy margin dear.

More than this ; — thy name reminds me
 Of three friends, all true and tried ;
And that name, like magic, binds me
 Closer, closer, to thy side.

Friends my soul with joy remembers !
 How like quivering flames they start,
When I fan the living embers
 On the hearth-stone of my heart !

'T is for this, thou Silent River !
 That my spirit leans to thee ;
Thou hast been a generous giver,
 Take this idle song from me.

THE GOBLET OF LIFE.

FILLED is Life's goblet to the brim ;
 And though my eyes with tears are dim,
I see its sparkling bubbles swim,
And chant a melancholy hymn
 With solemn voice and slow.

No purple flowers, — no garlands green,
Conceal the goblet's shade or sheen,
Nor maddening draughts of Hippocrene,
Like gleams of sunshine, flash between
 Thick leaves of mistletoe.

This goblet, wrought with curious art,
Is filled with waters, that upstart,
When the deep fountains of the heart,
By strong convulsions rent apart,
 Are running all to waste.

2

And as it mantling passes round,
With fennel is it wreathed and crowned,
Whose seed and foliage sun-imbrowned
Are in its waters steeped and drowned,
    And give a bitter taste.

Above the lowly plants it towers,
The fennel, with its yellow flowers,
And in an earlier age than ours
Was gifted with the wondrous powers,
    Lost vision to restore.

It gave new strength, and fearless mood;
And gladiators, fierce and rude,
Mingled it in their daily food;
And he who battled and subdued,
    A wreath of fennel wore.

Then in Life's goblet freely press,
The leaves that give it bitterness,
Nor prize the colored waters less,
For in thy darkness and distress
    New light and strength they give!

And he who has not learned to know
How false its sparkling bubbles show,
How bitter are the drops of woe,
With which its brim may overflow,
    He has not learned to live.

The prayer of Ajax was for light;
Through all that dark and desperate fight,
The blackness of that noonday night,
He asked but the return of sight,
    To see his foeman's face.

Let our unceasing, earnest prayer
Be, too, for light, — for strength to bear
Our portion of the weight of care,
That crushes into dumb despair
    One half the human race.

O suffering, sad humanity!
O ye afflicted ones, who lie
Steeped to the lips in misery,
Longing, and yet afraid to die,
 Patient, though sorely tried!

I pledge you in this cup of grief,
Where floats the fennel's bitter leaf,
The Battle of our Life is brief,
The alarm, — the struggle, — the relief, —
 Then sleep we side by side.

MAIDENHOOD.

MAIDEN! with the meek, brown eyes,
 In whose orbs a shadow lies
Like the dusk in evening skies!

Thou whose locks outshine the sun,
Golden tresses, wreathed in one,
As the braided streamlets run!

Standing, with reluctant feet,
Where the brook and river meet,
Womanhood and childhood fleet!

Gazing, with a timid glance,
On the brooklet's swift advance,
On the river's broad expanse!

Deep and still, that gliding stream
Beautiful to thee must seem,
As the river of a dream.

Then why pause with indecision,
When bright angels in thy vision
Beckon thee to fields Elysian?

Seest thou shadows sailing by,
As the dove, with startled eye,
Sees the falcon's shadow fly?

Hearest thou voices on the shore,
That our ears perceive no more,
Deafened by the cataract's roar?

O, thou child of many prayers!
Life hath quicksands, — Life hath snares, —
Care and age come unawares!

Like the swell of some sweet tune,
Morning rises into noon,
May glides onward into June.

Childhood is the bough, where slumbered
Birds and blossoms many-numbered; —
Age, that bough with snows encumbered.

Gather, then, each flower that grows,
When the young heart overflows,
To embalm that tent of snows.

Bear a lily in thy hand;
Gates of brass cannot withstand
One touch of that magic wand.

Bear through sorrow, wrong, and ruth,
In thy heart the dew of youth,
On thy lips the smile of truth.

O, that dew, like balm, shall steal
Into wounds, that cannot heal,
Even as sleep our eyes doth seal;

And that smile, like sunshine, dart
Into many a sunless heart,
For a smile of God thou art.

THE shades of night were falling fast,
  As through an Alpine village passed
A youth, who bore, 'mid snow and ice,
A banner with the strange device,
     Excelsior!

His brow was sad; his eye beneath,
Flashed like a faulchion from its sheath,
And like a silver clarion rung
The accents of that unknown tongue,
     Excelsior!

In happy homes he saw the light
Of household fires gleam warm and bright;
Above, the spectral glaciers shone,
And from his lips escaped a groan,
     Excelsior!

"Try not the Pass!" the old man said;
"Dark lowers the tempest overhead,
The roaring torrent is deep and wide!"
And loud that clarion voice replied,
          Excelsior!

"O stay," the maiden said, "and rest .
Thy weary head upon this breast!"
A tear stood in his bright blue eye,
But still he answered, with a sigh,
          Excelsior!

"Beware the pine-tree's withered branch!
Beware the awful avalanche!"
This was the peasant's last Good-night,
A voice replied, far up the height,
          Excelsior!

At break of day, as heavenward
The pious monks of Saint Bernard
Uttered the oft-repeated prayer,
A voice cried through the startled air,
          Excelsior!

A traveller, by the faithful hound,
Half-buried in the snow was found,
Still grasping in his hand of ice
That banner with the strange device,
          Excelsior!

There in the twilight cold and gray,
Lifeless, but beautiful, he lay,
And from the sky, serene and far,
A voice fell, like a falling star,
          Excelsior!

A GLEAM OF SUNSHINE.

THIS is the place.   Stand still, my steed,
    Let me review the scene,
And summon from the shadowy Past
    The forms that once have been.

The Past and Present here unite
    Beneath Time's flowing tide,
Like footprints hidden by a brook,
    But seen on either side.

Here runs the highway to the town;
    There the green lane descends,
Through which I walked to church with thee,
    O gentlest of my friends!

The shadow of the linden-trees,
    Lay moving on the grass;
Between them and the moving boughs,
    A shadow, thou didst pass.

Thy dress was like the lilies,
    And thy heart as pure as they:
One of God's holy messengers
    Did walk with me that day.

I saw the branches of the trees
    Bend down thy touch to meet,
The clover-blossoms in the grass
    Rise up to kiss thy feet.

"Sleep, sleep to-day, tormenting cares,
    Of earth and folly born!"
Solemnly sang the village choir
    On that sweet Sabbath morn.

Through the closed blinds the golden sun
　　Poured in a dusty beam,
Like the celestial ladder seen
　　By Jacob in his dream.

And ever and anon, the wind,
　　Sweet-scented with the hay,
Turned o'er the hymn-book's fluttering leaves
　　That on the window lay.

Long was the good man's sermon,
　　Yet it seemed not so to me;
For he spake of Ruth the beautiful,
　　And still I thought of thee.

Long was the prayer he uttered,
　　Yet it seemed not so to me;
For in my heart I prayed with him,
　　And still I thought of thee.

But now, alas! the place seems changed;
　　Thou art no longer here:
Part of the sunshine of the scene
　　With thee did disappear.

Though thoughts, deep-rooted in my heart,
　　Like pine-trees dark and high,
Subdue the light of noon, and breathe
　　A low and ceaseless sigh;

This memory brightens o'er the past,
　　As when the sun, concealed
Behind some cloud that near us hangs,
　　Shines on a distant field.

RAIN IN SUMMER.

HOW beautiful is the rain!
  After the dust and heat,
In the broad and fiery street,
In the narrow lane,
How beautiful is the rain!

How it clatters along the roofs,
Like the tramp of hoofs!
How it gushes and struggles out
From the throat of the overflowing spout!
Across the window-pane
It pours and pours;
And swift and wide,
With a muddy tide,
Like a river down the gutter roars
The rain, the welcome rain!

The sick man from his chamber looks
At the twisted brooks;
He can feel the cool
Breath of each little pool;
His fevered brain
Grows calm again,
And he breathes a blessing on the rain.

From the neighboring school
Come the boys,
With more than their wonted noise
And commotion;
And down the wet streets
Sail their mimic fleets,
Till the treacherous pool
Engulfs them in its whirling
And turbulent ocean.

2 *   c

In the country, on every side,
Where, far and wide,
Like a leopard's tawny and spotted hide,
Stretches the plain,
To the dry grass and the drier grain
How welcome is the rain!

In the furrowed land
The toilsome and patient oxen stand;
Lifting the yoke-encumbered head,
With their dilated nostrils spread,
They silently inhale
The clover-scented gale,
And the vapors that arise
From the well watered and smoking soil.
For this rest in the furrow after toil
Their large and lustrous eyes
Seem to thank the Lord,
More than man's spoken word.

Near at hand,
From under the sheltering trees,
The farmer sees
His pastures, and his fields of grain,
As they bend their tops
To the numberless beating drops
Of the incessant rain.
He counts it as no sin
That he sees therein
Only his own thrift and gain.
These, and far more than these,
The Poet sees!
He can behold
Aquarius old
Walking the fenceless fields of air;
And from each ample fold
Of the clouds about him rolled
Scattering everywhere
The showery rain,
As the farmer scatters his grain.

He can behold
Things manifold
That have not yet been wholly told,
Have not been wholly sung nor said.
For his thought, that never stops,
Follows the water-drops
Down to the graves of the dead,
Down through chasms and gulfs profound,
To the dreary fountain-head
Of lakes and rivers under ground;
And sees them, when the rain is done,
On the bridge of colors seven
Climbing up once more to heaven,
Opposite the setting sun.

Thus the Seer,
With vision clear,
Sees forms appear and disappear,
In the perpetual round of strange,
Mysterious change
From birth to death, from death to birth,
From earth to heaven, from heaven to earth;
Till glimpses more sublime
Of things, unseen before,
Unto his wondering eyes reveal
The Universe, as an immeasurable wheel
Turning forevermore
In the rapid and rushing river of Time.

TO A CHILD.

DEAR child! how radiant on thy mother's knee,
   With merry-making eyes and jocund smiles,
Thou gazest at the painted tiles,
Whose figures grace,
With many a grotesque form and face,

The ancient chimney of thy nursery!
The lady with the gay macaw,
The dancing girl, the grave bashaw
With bearded lip and chin;
And, leaning idly o'er his gate,
Beneath the imperial fan of state,
The Chinese mandarin.

With what a look of proud command
Thou shakest in thy little hand
The coral rattle with its silver bells,
Making a merry tune!
Thousands of years in Indian seas
That coral grew, by slow degrees,
Until some deadly and wild monsoon
Dashed it on Coromandel's sand!
Those silver bells
Reposed of yore,
As shapeless ore,
Far down in the deep-sunken wells
Of darksome mines,
In some obscure and sunless place,
Beneath huge Chimborazo's base,
Or Potosí's o'erhanging pines!
And thus for thee, O little child,
Through many a danger and escape,
The tall ships passed the stormy cape;
For thee in foreign lands remote,
Beneath the burning, tropic clime,
The Indian peasant, chasing the wild goat,
Himself as swift and wild,
In falling, clutched the frail arbute,
The fibres of whose shallow root,
Uplifted from the soil, betrayed
The silver veins beneath it laid,
The buried treasures of the pirate, Time.

But, lo! thy door is left ajar!
Thou hearest footsteps from afar!

And, at the sound,
Thou turnest round
With quick and questioning eyes,
Like one, who, in a foreign land,
Beholds on every hand
Some source of wonder and surprise!
And, restlessly, impatiently,
Thou strivest, strugglest, to be free.
The four walls of thy nursery
Are now like prison walls to thee.
No more thy mother's smiles,
No more the painted tiles,
Delight thee, nor the playthings on the floor
That won thy little, beating heart before;
Thou strugglest for the open door.

Through these once solitary halls
Thy pattering footstep falls.
The sound of thy merry voice
Makes the old walls
Jubilant, and they rejoice
With the joy of thy young heart,
O'er the light of whose gladness
No shadows of sadness
From the sombre background of memory start.

Once, ah, once, within these walls,
One whom memory oft recalls,
The Father of his Country, dwelt.
And yonder meadows, broad and damp,
The fires of the besieging camp
Encircled with a burning belt.
Up and down these echoing stairs,
Heavy with the weight of cares,
Sounded his majestic tread;
Yes, within this very room
Sat he in those hours of gloom,
Weary both in heart and head.

But what are these grave thoughts to thee?
Out, out! into the open air!
Thy only dream is liberty,
Thou carest little how or where.
I see thee eager at thy play,
Now shouting to the apples on the tree,
With cheeks as round and red as they;
And now among the yellow stalks,
Among the flowering shrubs and plants,
As restless as the bee.
Along the garden walks,
The tracks of thy small carriage-wheels I trace;
And see at every turn how they efface
Whole villages of sand-roofed tents,
That rise like golden domes
Above the cavernous and secret homes
Of wandering and nomadic tribes of ants.
Ah, cruel little Tamerlane,
Who, with thy dreadful reign,
Dost persecute and overwhelm
These hapless Troglodytes of thy realm!

What! tired already! with those suppliant looks,
And voice more beautiful than a poet's books,
Or murmuring sound of water as it flows,
Thou comest back to parley with repose!

TO A CHILD.

This rustic seat in the old apple-tree,
With its o'erhanging golden canopy
Of leaves illuminate with autumnal hues,
And shining with the argent light of dews,
Shall for a season be our place of rest.
Beneath us, like an oriole's pendent nest,
From which the laughing birds have taken wing,
By thee abandoned, hangs thy vacant swing.
Dream-like the waters of the river gleam;
A sailless vessel drops adown the stream,
And like it, to a sea as wide and deep,
Thou driftest gently down the tides of sleep.

O child! O new-born denizen
Of life's great city! on thy head
The glory of the morn is shed,
Like a celestial benison!
Here at the portal thou dost stand,
And with thy little hand
Thou openest the mysterious gate
Into the future's undiscovered land.
I see its valves expand,
As at the touch of Fate!
Into those realms of love and hate,
Into that darkness, blank and drear,
By some prophetic feeling taught,
I launch the bold, adventurous thought,
Freighted with hope and fear;
As upon subterranean streams,
In caverns unexplored and dark,
Men sometimes launch a fragile bark,
Laden with flickering fire,
And watch its swift-receding beams,
Until at length they disappear,
And in the distant dark expire.
By what astrology of fear or hope
Dare I to cast thy horoscope!
Like the new moon thy life appears;
A little strip of silver light,

And widening outward into night
The shadowy disk of future years;
And yet upon its outer rim,
A luminous circle, faint and dim,
And scarcely visible to us here,
Rounds and completes the perfect sphere;
A prophecy and intimation,
A pale and feeble adumbration,
Of the great world of light, that lies
Behind all human destinies.

Ah! if thy fate, with anguish fraught,
Should be to wet the dusty soil
With the hot tears and sweat of toil, —
To struggle with imperious thought,
Until the overburdened brain,
Weary with labor, faint with pain,
Like a jarred pendulum, retain
Only its motion, not its power, —
Remember, in that perilous hour,
When most afflicted and oppressed,
From labor there shall come forth rest.

And if a more auspicious fate
On thy advancing steps await,
Still let it ever be thy pride
To linger by the laborer's side;
With words of sympathy or song
To cheer the dreary march along
Of the great army of the poor,
O'er desert sand, o'er dangerous moor.

Nor to thyself the task shall be
Without reward; for thou shalt learn
The wisdom early to discern
True beauty in utility;
As great Pythagoras of yore,
Standing beside the blacksmith's door,
And hearing the hammers, as they smote

The anvils with a different note,
Stole from the varying tones, that hung
Vibrant on every iron tongue,
The secret of the sounding wire,
And formed the seven-chorded lyre.

Enough! I will not play the Seer;
I will no longer strive to ope
The mystic volume, where appear
The herald Hope, forerunning Fear,
And Fear, the pursuivant of Hope.
Thy destiny remains untold;
For, like Acestes' shaft of old,
The swift thought kindles as it flies,
And burns to ashes in the skies.

THE BRIDGE.

I STOOD on the bridge at midnight,
  As the clocks were striking the hour,
And the moon rose o'er the city,
  Behind the dark church-tower.

I saw her bright reflection
  In the waters under me,
Like a golden goblet falling
  And sinking into the sea.

And far in the hazy distance
  Of that lovely night in June,
The blaze of the flaming furnace
  Gleamed redder than the moon.

Among the long, black rafters
  The wavering shadows lay,
And the current that came from the ocean
  Seemed to lift and bear them away;

As, sweeping and eddying through them,
  Rose the belated tide,
And, streaming into the moonlight,
  The sea-weed floated wide.

And like those waters rushing
  Among the wooden piers,
A flood of thoughts came o'er me
  That filled my eyes with tears.

How often, O, how often,
  In the days that had gone by,
I had stood on that bridge at midnight
  And gazed on that wave and sky!

How often, O, how often,
  I had wished that the ebbing tide
Would bear me away on its bosom
  O'er the ocean wild and wide!

For my heart was hot and restless,
  And my life was full of care,
And the burden laid upon me
  Seemed greater than I could bear.

But now it has fallen from me,
  It is buried in the sea;
And only the sorrow of others
  Throws it shadow over me.

Yet whenever I cross the river
  On its bridge with wooden piers,
Like the odor of brine from the ocean
  Comes the thought of other years.

And I think how many thousands
  Of care-encumbered men,
Each bearing his burden of sorrow,
  Have crossed the bridge since then.

I see the long procession
   Still passing to and fro,
The young heart hot and restless,
   And the old subdued and slow !

And forever and forever,
   As long as the river flows,
As long as the heart has passions,
   As long as life has woes ;

The moon and its broken reflection
   And its shadows shall appear,
As the symbol of love in heaven,
   And its wavering image here.

SEA-WEED.

WHEN descends on the Atlantic
     The gigantic
Storm-wind of the equinox,
Landward in his wrath he scourges
     The toiling surges,
Laden with sea-weed from the rocks :

From Bermuda's reefs ; from edges
     Of sunken ledges,
In some far-off, bright Azore ;
From Bahama, and the dashing,
     Silver-flashing
Surges of San Salvador ;

From the tumbling surf, that buries
     The Orkneyan skerries,
Answering the hoarse Hebrides ;
And from wrecks of ships, and drifting
     Spars, uplifting
On the desolate, rainy seas ; —

Ever drifting, drifting, drifting
    On the shifting
Currents of the restless main ;
Till in sheltered coves, and reaches
    Of sandy beaches,
All have found repose again.

So when storms of wild emotion
    Strike the ocean
Of the poet's soul, erelong
From each cave and rocky fastness,
    In its vastness,
Floats some fragment of a song :

From the far-off isles enchanted,
    Heaven has planted
With the golden fruit of Truth ;
From the flashing surf, whose vision
    Gleams Elysian
In the tropic clime of Youth ;

From the strong Will, and the Endeavor
    That forever
Wrestles with the tides of Fate ;
From the wreck of Hopes far-scattered,
    Tempest-shattered,
Floating waste and desolate ; —

Ever drifting, drifting, drifting
    On the shifting
Currents of the restless heart ;
Till at length in books recorded,
    They, like hoarded
Household words, no more depart.

AFTERNOON IN FEBRUARY.

THE day is ending,
   The night is descending;
The marsh is frozen,
   The river dead.

Through clouds like ashes
The red sun flashes
On village windows
   That glimmer red.

The snow recommences;
The buried fences
Mark no longer
   The road o'er the plain;

While through the meadows,
Like fearful shadows,
Slowly passes
   A funeral train.

The bell is pealing,
And every feeling
Within me responds
   To the dismal knell;

Shadows are trailing,
My heart is bewailing
And tolling within
   Like a funeral bell.

THE DAY IS DONE.

THE day is done, and the darkness
   Falls from the wings of Night,
As a feather is wafted downward
   From an eagle in his flight.

I see the lights of the village
   Gleam through the rain and the mist,
And a feeling of sadness comes o'er me,
   That my soul cannot resist:

A feeling of sadness and longing,
   That is not akin to pain,
And resembles sorrow only
   As the mist resembles the rain.

Come, read to me some poem,
   Some simple and heartfelt lay,
That shall soothe this restless feeling,
   And banish the thoughts of day.

Not from the grand old masters,
  Not from the bards sublime,
Whose distant footsteps echo
  Through the corridors of Time.

For, like strains of martial music,
  Their mighty thoughts suggest
Life's endless toil and endeavor;
  And to-night I long for rest.

Read from some humbler poet,
  Whose songs gushed from his heart,
As showers from the clouds of summer,
  Or tears from the eyelids start;

Who, through long days of labor,
  And nights devoid of ease,
Still heard in his soul the music
  Of wonderful melodies.

Such songs have power to quiet
  The restless pulse of care,
And come like the benediction
  That follows after prayer.

Then read from the treasured volume
  The poem of thy choice,
And lend to the rhyme of the poet
  The beauty of thy voice.

And the night shall be filled with music,
  And the cares, that infest the day,
Shall fold their tents, like the Arabs,
  And as silently steal away.

THE ARROW AND THE SONG.

I SHOT an arrow into the air,
   It fell to earth, I knew not where;
For, so swiftly it flew, the sight
Could not follow it in its flight.

I breathed a song into the air,
It fell to earth, I knew not where;
For who has sight so keen and strong,
That it can follow the flight of song?

Long, long afterward, in an oak
I found the arrow, still unbroke;
And the song, from beginning to end,
I found again in the heart of a friend.

THE OLD CLOCK ON THE STAIRS.

L'éternité est une pendule, dont le balancier dit et redit sans cesse ces
deux mots seulement, dans le silence des tombeaux : "Toujours ! jamais !
Jamais ! toujours ! "

JACQUES BRIDAINE.

SOMEWHAT back from the village street
   Stands the old-fashioned country-seat.
Across its antique portico
Tall poplar-trees their shadows throw,
And from its station in the hall
An ancient timepiece says to all, —
     "Forever — never!
     Never — forever!"

Half-way up the stairs it stands,
And points and beckons with its hands
From its case of massive oak,
Like a monk, who, under his cloak,
Crosses himself, and sighs, alas!
With sorrowful voice to all who pass, —
    " Forever — never!
    Never — forever!"
3   D

By day its voice is low and light;
But in the silent dead of night,
Distinct as a passing footstep's fall,
It echoes along the vacant hall,
Along the ceiling, along the floor,
And seems to say, at each chamber-door, —
　　　" Forever — never!
　　　Never — forever!"

Through days of sorrow and of mirth,
Through days of death and days of birth,
Through every swift vicissitude
Of changeful time, unchanged it has stood,
And as if, like God, it all things saw,
It calmly repeats those words of awe, —
　　　" Forever — never!
　　　Never — forever!"

In that mansion used to be
Free-hearted Hospitality;
His great fires up the chimney roared;
The stranger feasted at his board;
But, like the skeleton at the feast,
That warning timepiece never ceased, —
　　　" Forever — never!
　　　Never — forever!"

There groups of merry children played,
There youths and maidens dreaming strayed.
O precious hours! O golden prime,
And affluence of love and time!
Even as a miser counts his gold,
Those hours the ancient timepiece told, —
　　　" Forever — never!
　　　Never — forever!"

From that chamber, clothed in white,
The bride came forth on her wedding night;
There, in that silent room below,
The dead lay in his shroud of snow;

And in the hush that followed the prayer,
Was heard the old clock on the stair, —
 "Forever — never!
 Never — forever!"

All are scattered now and fled,
Some are married, some are dead;
And when I ask, with throbs of pain,
"Ah! when shall they all meet again?
As in the days long-since gone by,
The ancient timepiece makes reply, —
 "Forever — never!
 Never — forever!"

Never here, forever there,
Where all parting, pain, and care,
And death, and time shall disappear, —
Forever there, but never here!
The horologe of Eternity
Sayeth this incessantly, —
 "Forever — never!
 Never — forever!"

THE EVENING STAR.

LO! in the painted oriel of the West,
 Whose panes the sunken sun incarnadines,
Like a fair lady at her casement, shines
The evening star, the star of love and rest!
And then anon she doth herself divest
Of all her radiant garments, and reclines
Behind the sombre screen of yonder pines,
With slumber and soft dreams of love oppressed.
O my beloved, my sweet Hesperus!
My morning and my evening star of love!

My best and gentlest lady! even thus,
As that fair planet in the sky above,
Dost thou retire unto thy rest at night,
And from thy darkened window fades the light.

AUTUMN.

THOU comest, Autumn, heralded by the rain,
    With banners, by great gales incessant fanned,
Brighter than brightest silks of Samarcand,
And stately oxen harnessed to thy wain!
Thou standest, like imperial Charlemagne,
Upon thy bridge of gold; thy royal hand
Outstretched with benedictions o'er the land,
Blessing the farms through all thy vast domain.
Thy shield is the red harvest moon, suspended
So long beneath the heaven's o'erhanging eaves,
Thy steps are by the farmer's prayers attended;
Like flames upon an altar shine the sheaves;
And, following thee, in thy ovation splendid,
Thine almoner, the wind, scatters the golden leaves!

THE SECRET OF THE SEA.

AH! what pleasant visions haunt me
    As I gaze upon the sea!
All the old romantic legends,
    All my dreams, come back to me.

Sails of silk and ropes of sendal,
    Such as gleam in ancient lore;
And the singing of the sailors,
    And the answer from the shore!

Most of all, the Spanish ballad
   Haunts me oft, and tarries long,
Of the noble Count Arnaldos
   And the sailor's mystic song.

Like the long waves on a sea-beach,
   Where the sand as silver shines,
With a soft, monotonous cadence,
   Flow its unrhymed lyric lines ; —

Telling how the Count Arnaldos,
   With his hawk upon his hand,
Saw a fair and stately galley,
   Steering onward to the land ; —

How he heard the ancient helmsman
   Chant a song so wild and clear,
That the sailing sea-bird slowly
   Poised upon the mast to hear,

Till his soul was full of longing,
   And he cried, with impulse strong, —
" Helmsman ! for the love of heaven,
   Teach me, too, that wondrous song ! "

" Wouldst thou," — so the helmsman answered,
   " Learn the secret of the sea ?
Only those who brave its dangers
   Comprehend its mystery ! "

In each sail that skims the horizon,
   In each landward-blowing breeze,
I behold that stately galley,
   Hear those mournful melodies ;

Till my soul is full of longing
   For the secret of the sea,
And the heart of the great ocean
   Sends a thrilling pulse through me.

TWILIGHT.

THE twilight is sad and cloudy,
    The wind blows wild and free,
And like the wings of sea-birds
    Flash the white caps of the sea.

But in the fisherman's cottage
    There shines a ruddier light,
And a little face at the window
    Peers out into the night.

Close, close it is pressed to the window,
    As if those childish eyes
Were looking into the darkness,
    To see some form arise.

And a woman's waving shadow
    Is passing to and fro,
Now rising to the ceiling,
    Now bowing and bending low.

What tale do the roaring ocean,
   And the night-wind, bleak and wild,
As they beat at the crazy casement,
   Tell to that little child?

And why do the roaring ocean,
   And the night-wind, wild and bleak,
As they beat at the heart of the mother,
   Drive the color from her cheek?

THE LIGHTHOUSE.

THE rocky ledge runs far into the sea,
   And on its outer point, some miles away,
The Lighthouse lifts its massive masonry,
   A pillar of fire by night, of cloud by day.

Even at this distance I can see the tides,
   Upheaving, break unheard along its base,
A speechless wrath, that rises and subsides
   In the white lip and tremor of the face.

And as the evening darkens, lo! how bright,
   Through the deep purple of the twilight air,
Beams forth the sudden radiance of its light,
   With strange, unearthly splendor in its glare!

Not one alone; from each projecting cape
   And perilous reef along the ocean's verge,
Starts into life a dim, gigantic shape,
   Holding its lantern o'er the restless surge.

Like the great giant Christopher it stands
   Upon the brink of the tempestuous wave,
Wading far out among the rocks and sands,
   The night-o'ertaken mariner to save.

And the great ships sail outward and return,
   Bending and bowing o'er the billowy swells,
And ever joyful, as they see it burn,
   They wave their silent welcomes and farewells.

They come forth from the darkness, and their sails
   Gleam for a moment only in the blaze,
And eager faces, as the light unveils,
   Gaze at the tower, and vanish while they gaze.

The mariner remembers when a child,
   On his first voyage, he saw it fade and sink;
And when, returning from adventures wild,
   He saw it rise again o'er ocean's brink.

Steadfast, serene, immovable, the same
   Year after year, through all the silent night,
Burns on forevermore that quenchless flame,
   Shines on that inextinguishable light!

It sees the ocean to its bosom clasp
   The rocks and sea-sand with the kiss of peace;
It sees the wild winds lift it in their grasp,
   And hold it up, and shake it like a fleece.

The startled waves leap over it; the storm
   Smites it with all the scourges of the rain,
And steadily against its solid form
   Press the great shoulders of the hurricane.

The sea-bird wheeling round it, with the din
   Of wings and winds and solitary cries,
Blinded and maddened by the light within,
   Dashes himself against the glare, and dies.

A new Prometheus, chained upon the rock,
   Still grasping in his hand the fire of Jove,
It does not hear the cry, nor heed the shock,
   But hails the mariner with words of love.

" Sail on ! " it says, " sail on, ye stately ships !
　And with your floating bridge the ocean span ;
Be mine to guard this light from all eclipse,
　Be yours to bring man nearer unto man ! "

THE FIRE OF DRIFT-WOOD.

WE sat within the farm-house old,
　　Whose windows, looking o'er the bay,
Gave to the sea-breeze, damp and cold,
　An easy entrance, night and day.

Not far away we saw the port, —
　The strange, old-fashioned, silent town, —
The lighthouse, the dismantled fort, —
　The wooden houses, quaint and brown.

We sat and talked until the night,
　Descending, filled the little room ;
Our faces faded from the sight,
　Our voices only broke the gloom.

We spake of many a vanished scene,
　Of what we once had thought and said,
Of what had been, and might have been,
　And who was changed, and who was dead ;

And all that fills the hearts of friends,
　When first they feel, with secret pain,
Their lives thenceforth have separate ends,
　And never can be one again ;

The first slight swerving of the heart,
　That words are powerless to express,
And leave it still unsaid in part,
　Or say it in too great excess.
　　3 *

The very tones in which we spake
    Had something strange, I could but mark;
The leaves of memory seemed to make
    A mournful rustling in the dark.

Oft died the words upon our lips,
    As suddenly, from out the fire
Built of the wreck of stranded ships,
    The flames would leap and then expire.

And, as their splendor flashed and failed,
    We thought of wrecks upon the main, —
Of ships dismasted, that were hailed
    And sent no answer back again.

The windows, rattling in their frames, —
    The ocean, roaring up the beach, —
The gusty blast, — the bickering flames, —
    All mingled vaguely in our speech;

Until they made themselves a part
    Of fancies floating through the brain, —
The long-lost ventures of the heart,
    That send no answers back again.

O flames that glowed! O hearts that yearned!
    They were indeed too much akin,
The drift-wood fire without that burned,
    The thoughts that burned and glowed within.

RESIGNATION.

THERE is no flock, however watched and tended,
But one dead lamb is there!
There is no fireside, howsoe'er defended,
But has one vacant chair!

The air is full of farewells to the dying,
And mournings for the dead;
The heart of Rachel, for her children crying,
Will not be comforted!

Let us be patient! These severe afflictions
Not from the ground arise,
But oftentimes celestial benedictions
Assume this dark disguise.

We see but dimly through the mists and vapors;
Amid these earthly damps,
What seem to us but sad, funereal tapers
May be heaven's distant lamps.

There is no Death! What seems so is transition.
This life of mortal breath
Is but a suburb of the life elysian,
Whose portal we call Death.

She is not dead, — the child of our affection, —
But gone unto that school
Where she no longer needs our poor protection,
And Christ himself doth rule.

In that great cloister's stillness and seclusion,
By guardian angels led,
Safe from temptation, safe from sin's pollution,
She lives, whom we call dead.

Day after day we think what she is doing
  In those bright realms of air;
Year after year, her tender steps pursuing,
  Behold her grown more fair.

Thus do we walk with her, and keep unbroken
  The bond which nature gives,
Thinking that our remembrance, though unspoken,
  May reach her where she lives.

Not as a child shall we again behold her;
  For when with raptures wild
In our embraces we again enfold her,
  She will not be a child;

But a fair maiden, in her Father's mansion,
  Clothed with celestial grace;
And beautiful with all the soul's expansion
  Shall we behold her face.

And though at times impetuous with emotion
  And anguish long suppressed,
The swelling heart heaves moaning like the ocean,
  That cannot be at rest, —

We will be patient, and assuage the feeling
  We may not wholly stay;
By silence sanctifying, not concealing,
  The grief that must have way.

THE BUILDERS.

ALL are architects of Fate,
    Working in these walls of Time;
Some with massive deeds and great,
    Some with ornaments of rhyme.

Nothing useless is, or low;
    Each thing in its place is best;
And what seems but idle show
    Strengthens and supports the rest.

For the structure that we raise,
   Time is with materials filled ;
Our to-days and yesterdays
   Are the blocks with which we build.

Truly shape and fashion these ;
   Leave no yawning gaps between ;
Think not, because no man sees,
   Such things will remain unseen.

In the elder days of Art,
   Builders wrought with greatest care
Each minute and unseen part ;
   For the Gods see everywhere.

Let us do our work as well,
   Both the unseen and the seen ;
Make the house, where Gods may dwell,
   Beautiful, entire, and clean.

Else our lives are incomplete,
   Standing in these walls of Time,
Broken stairways, where the feet
   Stumble as they seek to climb.

Build to-day, then, strong and sure,
   With a firm and ample base ;
And ascending and secure
   Shall to-morrow find its place.

Thus alone can we attain
   To those turrets, where the eye
Sees the world as one vast plain,
   And one boundless reach of sky.

THE OPEN WINDOW.

THE old house by the lindens
   Stood silent in the shade,
And on the gravelled pathway
   The light and shadow played.

I saw the nursery windows
   Wide open to the air;
But the faces of the children,
   They were no longer there.

The large Newfoundland house-dog
　Was standing by the door;
He looked for his little playmates,
　Who would return no more.

They walked not under the lindens,
　They played not in the hall;
But shadow, and silence, and sadness
　Were hanging over all.

The birds sang in the branches,
　With sweet, familiar tone;
But the voices of the children
　Will be heard in dreams alone!

And the boy that walked beside me,
　He could not understand
Why closer in mine, ah! closer,
　I pressed his warm, soft hand!

SUSPIRIA.

TAKE them, O Death! and bear away
　Whatever thou canst call thine own!
Thine image, stamped upon this clay,
　Doth give thee that, but that alone!

Take them, O Grave! and let them lie
　Folded upon thy narrow shelves,
As garments by the soul laid by,
　And precious only to ourselves!

Take them, O great Eternity!
　Our little life is but a gust,
That bends the branches of thy tree,
　And trails its blossoms in the dust.

THE LADDER OF ST. AUGUSTINE.

SAINT AUGUSTINE! well hast thou said, ·
 That of our vices we can frame
A ladder, if we will but tread
 Beneath our feet each deed of shame!

All common things, each day's events,
 That with the hour begin and end,
Our pleasures and our discontents,
 Are rounds by which we may ascend.

The low desire, the base design,
 That makes another's virtues less;
The revel of the ruddy wine,
 And all occasions of excess;

The longing for ignoble things;
 The strife for triumph more than truth;
The hardening of the heart, that brings
 Irreverence for the dreams of youth;

All thoughts of ill; all evil deeds,
 That have their root in thoughts of ill;
Whatever hinders or impedes
 The action of the nobler will; —

All these must first be trampled down
 Beneath our feet, if we would gain
In the bright fields of fair renown
 The right of eminent domain.

We have not wings, we cannot soar;
 But we have feet to scale and climb
By slow degrees, by more and more,
 The cloudy summits of our time.

E

The mighty pyramids of stone
  That wedge-like cleave the desert airs,
When nearer seen, and better known,
  Are but gigantic flights of stairs.

The distant mountains, that uprear
  Their solid bastions to the skies,
Are crossed by pathways, that appear
  As we to higher levels rise.

The heights by great men reached and kept,
  Were not attained by sudden flight,
But they, while their companions slept,
  Were toiling upward in the night.

Standing on what too long we bore
  With shoulders bent and downcast eyes,
We may discern — unseen before —
  A path to higher destinies.

Nor deem the irrevocable Past,
  As wholly wasted, wholly vain,
If, rising on its wrecks, at last
  To something nobler we attain.

HAUNTED HOUSES.

ALL houses wherein men have lived and died
  Are haunted houses. Through the open doors
The harmless phantoms on their errands glide,
  With feet that make no sound upon the floors.

We meet them at the door-way, on the stair,
  Along the passages they come and go,
Impalpable impressions on the air,
  A sense of something moving to and fro.

There are more guests at table, than the hosts
    Invited; the illuminated hall
Is thronged with quiet, inoffensive ghosts,
    As silent as the pictures on the wall.

The stranger at my fireside cannot see
    The forms I see, nor hear the sounds I hear;
He but perceives what is; while unto me
    All that has been is visible and clear.

We have no title-deeds to house or lands;
    Owners and occupants of earlier dates
From graves forgotten stretch their dusty hands,
    And hold in mortmain still their old estates.

The spirit-world around this world of sense
    Floats like an atmosphere, and everywhere
Wafts through these earthly mists and vapors dense
    A vital breath of more ethereal air.

Our little lives are kept in equipoise
    By opposite attractions and desires;
The struggle of the instinct that enjoys,
    And the more noble instinct that aspires.

These perturbations, this perpetual jar
    Of earthly wants and aspirations high,
Come from the influence of an unseen star,
    An undiscovered planet in our sky.

And as the moon from some dark gate of cloud
    Throws o'er the sea a floating bridge of light,
Across whose trembling planks our fancies crowd
    Into the realm of mystery and night, —

So from the world of spirits there descends
    A bridge of light, connecting it with this,
O'er whose unsteady floor, that sways and bends,
    Wander our thoughts above the dark abyss.

IN THE CHURCHYARD AT CAMBRIDGE.

I N the village churchyard she lies,
　Dust is in her beautiful eyes,
　　No more she breathes, nor feels, nor stirs;
At her feet and at her head
Lies a slave to attend the dead,
　　But their dust is white as hers.

Was she a lady of high degree,
So much in love with the vanity
　　And foolish pomp of this world of ours?
Or was it Christian charity,
And lowliness and humility,
　　The richest and rarest of all dowers?

Who shall tell us?　No one speaks;
No color shoots into those cheeks,
　　Either of anger or of pride,
At the rude question we have asked;
Nor will the mystery be unmasked
　　By those who are sleeping at her side.

Hereafter?— And do you think to look
On the terrible pages of that Book
　　To find her failings, faults, and errors?
Ah, you will then have other cares,
In your own short-comings and despairs,
　　In your own secret sins and terrors!

.

THE TWO ANGELS.

T WO angels, one of Life and one of Death,
　Passed o'er our village as the morning broke;
The dawn was on their faces, and beneath,
　The sombre houses hearsed with plumes of smoke.

Their attitude and aspect were the same,
　Alike their features and their robes of white;
But one was crowned with amaranth, as with flame,
　And one with asphodels, like flakes of light:

I saw them pause on their celestial way;
　Then said I, with deep fear and doubt oppressed,
" Beat not so loud, my heart, lest thou betray
　The place where thy beloved are at rest ! "

And he who wore the crown of asphodels,
　Descending, at my door began to knock,
And my soul sank within me, as in wells
　The waters sink before an earthquake's shock.

I recognized the nameless agony,
    The terror and the tremor and the pain,
That oft before had filled or haunted me,
    And now returned with threefold strength again.

The door I opened to my heavenly guest,
    And listened, for I thought I heard God's voice;
And, knowing whatsoe'er he sent was best,
    Dared neither to lament nor to rejoice.

Then with a smile, that filled the house with light,
    "My errand is not Death, but Life," he said;
And ere I answered, passing out of sight,
    On his celestial embassy he sped.

'T was at thy door, O friend! and not at mine,
    The angel with the amaranthine wreath,
Pausing, descended, and with voice divine,
    Whispered a word that had a sound like Death.

Then fell upon the house a sudden gloom,
    A shadow on those features fair and thin;
And softly, from that hushed and darkened room,
    Two angels issued, where but one went in.

All is of God! If he but wave his hand,
    The mists collect, the rain falls thick and loud,
Till, with a smile of light on sea and land,
    Lo! he looks back from the departing cloud.

Angels of Life and Death alike are his;
    Without his leave they pass no threshold o'er;
Who, then, would wish or dare, believing this,
    Against his messengers to shut the door?

DAYLIGHT AND MOONLIGHT.

IN broad daylight, and at noon,
  Yesterday I saw the moon
Sailing high, but faint and white,
As a schoolboy's paper kite.

In broad daylight, yesterday,
I read a Poet's mystic lay;
And it seemed to me at most
As a phantom, or a ghost.

But at length the feverish day
Like a passion died away,
And the night, serene and still,
Fell on village, vale, and hill.

Then the moon, in all her pride,
Like a spirit glorified,
Filled and overflowed the night
With revelations of her light.

And the Poet's song again
Passed like music through my brain;
Night interpreted to me
All its grace and mystery.

MY LOST YOUTH.

OFTEN I think of the beautiful town
  That is seated by the sea;
Often in thought go up and down
The pleasant streets of that dear old town,
  And my youth comes back to me.

And a verse of a Lapland song
Is haunting my memory still:
" A boy's will is the wind's will,
And the thoughts of youth are long, long thoughts."

I can see the shadowy lines of its trees,
And catch, in sudden gleams,
The sheen of the far-surrounding seas,
And islands that were the Hesperides
Of all my boyish dreams.
And the burden of that old song,
It murmurs and whispers still:
" A boy's will is the wind's will,
And the thoughts of youth are long, long thoughts."

I remember the black wharves and the slips,
And the sea-tides tossing free;
And Spanish sailors with bearded lips,
And the beauty and mystery of the ships,
And the magic of the sea.
And the voice of that wayward song
Is singing and saying still:
" A boy's will is the wind's will,
And the thoughts of youth are long, long thoughts."

I remember the bulwarks by the shore,
And the fort upon the hill;
The sun-rise gun, with its hollow roar,
The drum-beat repeated o'er and o'er,
And the bugle wild and shrill.
And the music of that old song
Throbs in my memory still:
" A boy's will is the wind's will,
And the thoughts of youth are long, long thoughts."

I remember the sea-fight far away,
How it thundered o'er the tide!
And the dead captains, as they lay
In their graves, o'erlooking the tranquil bay,
Where they in battle died.

And the sound of that mournful song
  Goes through me with a thrill :
" A boy's will is the wind's will,
And the thoughts of youth are long, long thoughts."

I can see the breezy dome of groves,
  The shadows of Deering's Woods ;
And the friendships old and the early loves
Came back with a Sabbath sound, as of doves
  In quiet neighborhoods.
    And the verse of that sweet old song,
    It flutters and murmurs still :
" A boy's will is the wind's will,
And the thoughts of youth are long, long thoughts."

I remember the gleams and glooms that dart
  Across the schoolboy's brain ;
The song and the silence in the heart,
That in part are prophecies, and in part
  Are longings wild and vain.
    And the voice of that fitful song
    Sings on, and is never still :
" A boy's will is the wind's will,
And the thoughts of youth are long, long thoughts."

There are things of which I may not speak ;
  There are dreams that cannot die ;
There are thoughts that make the strong heart weak,
And bring a pallor into the cheek,
  And a mist before the eye.
    And the words of that fatal song
    Come over me like a chill :
" A boy's' will is the wind's will,
And the thoughts of youth are long, long thoughts."

Strange to me now are the forms I meet
  When I visit the dear old town ;
But the native air is pure and sweet,
And the trees that o'ershadow each well-known street,
  As they balance up and down,

4

Are singing the beautiful song,
Are sighing and whispering still:
"A boy's will is the wind's will,
And the thoughts of youth are long, long thoughts."

And Deering's Woods are fresh and fair,
And with joy that is almost pain
My heart goes back to wander there,
And among the dreams of the days that were,
I find my lost youth again.
And the strange and beautiful song,
The groves are repeating it still:
"A boy's will is the wind's will,
And the thoughts of youth are long, long thoughts."

THE GOLDEN MILESTONE.

LEAFLESS are the trees; their purple branches
Spread themselves abroad, like reefs of coral,
Rising silent
In the Red Sea of the Winter sunset.

From the hundred chimneys of the village,
Like the Afreet in the Arabian story,
Smoky columns
Tower aloft into the air of amber.

At the window winks the flickering fire-light;
Here and there the lamps of evening glimmer,
Social watch-fires
Answering one another through the darkness.

On the hearth the lighted logs are glowing,
And like Ariel in the cloven pine-tree
For its freedom
Groans and sighs the air imprisoned in them.

By the fireside there are old men seated,
Seeing ruined cities in the ashes,
    Asking sadly
Of the Past what it can ne'er restore them.

By the fireside there are youthful dreamers,
Building castles fair, with stately stairways,
    Asking blindly
Of the Future what it cannot give them.

By the fireside tragedies are acted
In whose scenes appear two actors only,
    Wife and husband,
And above them God the sole spectator.

By the fireside there are peace and comfort,
Wives and children, with fair, thoughtful faces,
    Waiting, watching
For a well-known footstep in the passage.

Each man's chimney is his Golden Mile-stone;
Is the central point, from which he measures
    Every distance
Through the gateways of the world around him.

In his farthest wanderings still he sees it;
Hears the talking flame, the answering night-wind,
    As he heard them
When he sat with those who were, but are not.

Happy he whom neither wealth nor fashion,
Nor the march of the encroaching city,
    Drives an exile
From the hearth of his ancestral homestead.

We may build more splendid habitations,
Fill our rooms with paintings and with sculptures,
    But we cannot
Buy with gold the old associations!

DAYBREAK.

A WIND came up out of the sea,
And said, "O mists, make room for me."

It hailed the ships, and cried, "Sail on,
Ye mariners, the night is gone."

And hurried landward far away,
Crying, "Awake! it is the day."

It said unto the forest, "Shout!
Hang all your leafy banners out!"

It touched the wood-bird's folded wing,
And said, "O bird, awake and sing."

And o'er the farms, "O chanticleer,
Your clarion blow; the day is near."

It whispered to the fields of corn,
"Bow down, and hail the coming morn."

It shouted through the belfry-tower,
"Awake, O bell! proclaim the hour."

It crossed the churchyard with a sigh,
And said, "Not yet! in quiet lie."

THE ROPEWALK.

IN that building, long and low,
  With its windows all a-row,
Like the port-holes of a hulk,
Human spiders spin and spin,
Backward down their threads so thin
  Dropping, each a hempen bulk.

At the end, an open door;
Squares of sunshine on the floor
  Light the long and dusky lane;

And the whirring of a wheel,
Dull and drowsy, makes me feel
   All its spokes are in my brain.

As the spinners to the end
Downward go and reascend,
   Gleam the long threads in the sun;
While within this brain of mine
Cobwebs brighter and more fine
   By the busy wheel are spun.

Two fair maidens in a swing, ·
Like white doves upon the wing,
   First before my vision pass;
Laughing, as their gentle hands
Closely clasp the twisted strands,
   At their shadow on the grass.

Then a booth of mountebanks,
With its smell of tan and planks,
   And a girl poised high in air
On a cord, in spangled dress,
With a faded loveliness,
   And a weary look of care.

Then a homestead among farms,
And a woman with bare arms
   Drawing water from a well;
As the bucket mounts apace,
With it mounts her own fair face,
   As at some magician's spell.

Then an old man in a tower,
Ringing loud the noontide hour,
   While the rope coils round and round
Like a serpent at his feet,
And again, in swift retreat,
   Nearly lifts him from the ground.

Then within a prison-yard,
Faces fixed, and stern, and hard,
   Laughter and indecent mirth;
Ah! it is the gallows-tree!
Breath of Christian charity,
   Blow, and sweep it from the earth!

Then a school-boy, with his kite
Gleaming in a sky of light,
   And an eager, upward look;
Steeds pursued through lane and field;
Fowlers with their snares concealed;
   And an angler by a brook.

Ships rejoicing in the breeze,
Wrecks that float o'er unknown seas,
   Anchors dragged through faithless sand;
Sea-fog drifting overhead,
And, with lessening line and lead,
   Sailors feeling for the land.

All these scenes do I behold,
These, and many left untold,
   In that building long and low;
While the wheel goes round and round,
With a drowsy, dreamy sound,
   And the spinners backward go.

SANDALPHON.

HAVE you read in the Talmud of old,
   In the Legends the Rabbins have told
  Of the limitless realms of the air, —
Have you read it, — the marvellous story
Of Sandalphon, the Angel of Glory,
  Sandalphon, the Angel of Prayer?

How, erect, at the outermost gates
Of the City Celestial he waits,
  With his feet on the ladder of light,
That, crowded with angels unnumbered,
By Jacob was seen, as he slumbered
  Alone in the desert at night?   .

The Angels of Wind and of Fire
Chaunt only one hymn, and expire
  With the song's irresistible stress;
Expire in their rapture and wonder,
As harp-strings are broken asunder
  By music they throb to express.

But serene in the rapturous throng,
Unmoved by the rush of the song,
  With eyes unimpassioned and slow,
Among the dead angels, the deathless
Sandalphon stands listening breathless
  To sounds that ascend from below; —

From the spirits on earth that adore,
From the souls that entreat and implore
  In the fervor and passion of prayer;
From the hearts that are broken with losses,
And weary with dragging the crosses
  Too heavy for mortals to bear.

And he gathers the prayers as he stands,
And they change into flowers in his hands,
  Into garlands of purple and red;
And beneath the great arch of the portal,
Through the streets of the City Immortal
  Is wafted the fragrance they shed.

It is but a legend, I know, —
A fable, a phantom, a show,
  Of the ancient Rabbinical lore;
Yet the old mediæval tradition,
The beautiful, strange superstition,
  But haunts me and holds me the more.

When I look from my window at night,
And the welkin above is all white,
   All throbbing and panting with stars,
Among them majestic is standing
Sandalphon the angel, expanding
   His pinions in nebulous bars.

And the legend, I feel, is a part
Of the hunger and thirst of the heart,
   The frenzy and fire of the brain,
That grasps at the fruitage forbidden,
The golden pomegranates of Eden,
   To quiet its fever and pain.

THE CHILDREN'S HOUR.

B ETWEEN the dark and the daylight,
   When the night is beginning to lower,
Comes a pause in the day's occupations,
   That is known as the Children's Hour.

I hear in the chamber above me
   The patter of little feet,
The sound of a door that is opened,
   And voices soft and sweet.

From my study I see in the lamplight,
   Descending the broad hall stair,
Grave Alice, and laughing Allegra,
   And Edith with golden hair.

A whisper, and then a silence:
   Yet I know by their merry eyes
They are plotting and planning together
   To take me by surprise.

A sudden rush from the stairway,
  A sudden raid from the hall!
By three doors left unguarded
  They enter my castle wall!

They climb up into my turret
  O'er the arms and back of my chair;
If I try to escape, they surround me;
  They seem to be everywhere.

They almost devour me with kisses,
  Their arms about me entwine,
Till I think of the Bishop of Bingen
  In his Mouse-Tower on the Rhine!

Do you think, O blue-eyed banditti,
  Because you have scaled the wall,
Such an old moustache as I am
  Is not a match for you all!

I have you fast in my fortress,
  And will not let you depart,
But put you down into the dungeon
  In the round-tower of my heart.

And there will I keep you forever,
  Yes, forever and a day,
Till the walls shall crumble to ruin,
  And moulder in dust away!

SNOW-FLAKES.

OUT of the bosom of the Air,
  Out of the cloud-folds of her garments shaken,
Over the woodlands brown and bare,
  Over the harvest-fields forsaken,
    Silent, and soft, and slow
    Descends the snow.

Even as our cloudy fancies take
  Suddenly shape in some divine expression,
Even as the troubled heart doth make
  In the white countenance confession,
      The troubled sky reveals
      The grief it feels.

This is the poem of the air,
  Slowly in silent syllables recorded;
This is the secret of despair,
  Long in its cloudy bosom hoarded,
      Now whispered and revealed
      To wood and field.

A DAY OF SUNSHINE.

O GIFT of God! O perfect day:
  Whereon shall no man work, but play;
Whereon it is enough for me,
Not to be doing, but to be!

Through every fibre of my brain,
Through every nerve, through every vein,
I feel the electric thrill, the touch
Of life, that seems almost too much.

I hear the wind among the trees
Playing celestial symphonies;
I see the branches downward bent,
Like keys of some great instrument.

And over me unrolls on high
The splendid scenery of the sky,
Where through a sapphire sea the sun
Sails like a golden galleon,

Towards yonder cloud-land in the West,
Towards yonder Islands of the Blest,
Whose steep sierra far uplifts
Its craggy summits white with drifts.

Blow, winds! and waft through all the rooms
The snow-flakes of the cherry-blooms!
Blow, winds! and bend within my reach
The fiery blossoms of the peach!

O Life and Love!   O happy throng
Of thoughts, whose only speech is song!
O heart of man! canst thou not be
Blithe as the air is, and as free?

SOMETHING LEFT UNDONE.

LABOR with what zeal we will,
    Something still remains undone,
Something uncompleted still
    Waits the rising of the sun.

By the bedside, on the stair,
    At the threshold, near the gates,
With its menace or its prayer,
    Like a mendicant it waits;

Waits, and will not go away;
    Waits, and will not be gainsaid;
By the cares of yesterday
    Each to-day is heavier made;

Till at length the burden seems
    Greater than our strength can bear,
Heavy as the weight of dreams,
    Pressing on us everywhere.

And we stand from day to day,
   Like the dwarfs of times gone by,
Who, as Northern legends say,
   On their shoulders held the sky.

WEARINESS.

O LITTLE feet! that such long years
   Must wander on through hopes and fears,
Must ache and bleed beneath your load;
I, nearer to the wayside inn
Where toil shall cease and rest begin,
   Am weary, thinking of your road!

O little hands! that, weak or strong,
Have still to serve or rule so long,
   Have still so long to give or ask;
I, who so much with book and pen
Have toiled among my fellow-men,
   Am weary, thinking of your task.

O little hearts! that throb and beat
With such impatient, feverish heat,
   Such limitless and strong desires;
Mine that so long has glowed and burned,
With passions into ashes turned
   Now covers and conceals its fires.

O little souls! as pure and white
And crystalline as rays of light
   Direct from heaven, their source divine;
Refracted through the mist of years,
How red my setting sun appears,
   How lurid looks this soul of mine!

CHILDREN.

COME to me, O ye children !
   For I hear you at your play,
And the questions that perplexed me
   Have vanished quite away.

Ye open the eastern windows,
    That look towards the sun,
Where thoughts are singing swallows
    And the brooks of morning run.

In your hearts are the birds and the sunshine,.
    In your thoughts the brooklet's flow,
But in mine is the wind of Autumn
    And the first fall of the snow.   .

Ah! what would the world be to us
    If the children were no more?
We should dread the desert behind us
    Worse than the dark before.

What the leaves are to the forest,
    With light and air for food,
Ere their sweet and tender juices
    Have been hardened into wood, —

That to the world are children;
    Through them it feels the glow
Of a brighter and sunnier climate
    Than reaches the trunks below.

Come to me, O ye children!
    And whisper in my ear
What the birds and the winds are singing
    In your sunny atmosphere.

For what are all our contrivings,
    And the wisdom of our books,
When compared with your caresses,
    And the gladness of your looks?

Ye are better than all the ballads
    That ever were sung or said;
For ye are living poems,
    And all the rest are dead.

.

THE BRIDGE OF CLOUD.

BURN, O evening hearth, and waken
   Pleasant visions, as of old!
Though the house by winds be shaken,
. Safe I keep this room of gold!

Ah! no longer wizard Fancy
   Builds its castles in the air,
Luring me by necromancy
   Up the never-ending stair.

But, instead, it builds me bridges
   Over many a dark ravine,
Where beneath the gusty ridges
   Cataracts dash and roar unseen.

And I cross them, little heeding
   Blast of wind or torrent's roar,
As I follow the receding
   Footsteps that have gone before.

Naught avails the imploring gesture,
   Naught avails the cry of pain!
When I touch the flying vesture,
   'T is the gray robe of the rain.

Baffled I return, and, leaning
   O'er the parapets of cloud,
Watch the mist that intervening
   Wraps the valley in its shroud.

And the sounds of life ascending
   Faintly, vaguely, meet the ear,
Murmur of bells and voices blending
   With the rush of waters near.

Well I know what there lies hidden,
    Every tower and town and farm,
And again the land forbidden
    Reassumes its vanished charm.

Well I know the secret places,
    And the nests in hedge and tree ;
At what doors are friendly faces,
    In what hearts a thought of me.

Through the mist and darkness sinking,
    Blown by wind and beaten by shower,
Down I fling the thought I 'm thinking,
    Down I toss this Alpine flower.

PALINGENESIS.

I LAY upon the headland-height, and listened
    To the incessant sobbing of the sea
      In caverns under me,
And watched the waves, that tossed and fled and glistened,
Until the rolling meadows of amethyst
    Melted away in mist.

Then suddenly, as one from sleep, I started ;
For round about me all the sunny capes
    Seemed peopled with the shapes
Of those whom I had known in days departed,
Apparelled in the loveliness which gleams
    On faces seen in dreams.

A moment only, and the light and glory
Faded away, and the disconsolate shore
    Stood lonely as before ;
And the wild roses of the promontory
Around me shuddered in the wind, and shed
    Their petals of pale red.

There was an old belief that in the embers
Of all things their primordial form exists,
   And cunning alchemists
Could recreate the rose with all its members
From its own ashes, but without the bloom,
   Without the lost perfume.

Ah me! what wonder-working, occult science
Can from the ashes in our hearts once more
   The rose of youth restore?
What craft of alchemy can bid defiance
To time and change, and for a single hour
   Renew this phantom-flower?

"O, give me back," I cried, "the vanished splendors,
The breath of morn, and the exultant strife,
   When the swift stream of life
Bounds o'er its rocky channel, and surrenders
The pond, with all its lilies, for the leap
   Into the unknown deep!"

And the sea answered, with a lamentation,
Like some old prophet wailing, and it said,
   "Alas! thy youth is dead!
It breathes no more, its heart has no pulsation,
In the dark places with the dead of old
   It lies forever cold!"

Then said I, "From its consecrated cerements
I will not drag this sacred dust again,
   Only to give me pain;
But, still remembering all the lost endearments,
Go on my way, like one who looks before,
   And turns to weep no more."

Into what land of harvests, what plantations
Bright with autumnal foliage and the glow
   Of sunsets burning low;

Beneath what midnight skies, whose constellations
Light up the spacious avenues between
    This world and the unseen!

Amid what friendly greetings and caresses,
What households, though not alien, yet not mine,
    What bowers of rest divine;
To what temptations in lone wildernesses,
What famine of the heart, what pain and loss,
    The bearing of what cross

I do not know; nor will I vainly question
Those pages of the mystic book which hold
    The story still untold,
But without rash conjecture or suggestion
Turn its last leaves in reverence and good heed,
    Until "The End" I read.

THE BROOK.

FROM THE SPANISH.

LAUGH of the mountain!—lyre of bird and tree!
    Pomp of the meadow! mirror of the morn!
The soul of April, unto whom are born
The rose and jessamine, leaps wild in thee!
Although, where'er thy devious current strays,
The lap of earth with gold and silver teems,
To me thy clear proceeding brighter seems
Than golden sands, that charm each shepherd's gaze.
How without guile thy bosom, all transparent
As the pure crystal, lets the curious eye
Thy secrets scan, thy smooth, round pebbles count!
How, without malice murmuring, glides thy current!
O sweet simplicity of days gone by!
Thou shun'st the haunts of man, to dwell in limpid fount!

SONG OF THE SILENT LAND.

FROM THE GERMAN OF SALIS.

INTO the Silent Land!
  Ah! who shall lead us thither?
Clouds in the evening sky more darkly gather,
And shattered wrecks lie thicker on the strand.
Who leads us with a gentle hand
Thither, O thither,
Into the Silent Land?

Into the Silent Land!
To you, ye boundless regions
Of all perfection!   Tender morning visions
Of beauteous souls!   The Future's pledge and band
Who in Life's battle firm doth stand,
Shall bear Hope's tender blossoms
Into the Silent Land!

O Land!   O Land!
For all the broken-hearted
The mildest herald by our fate allotted,
Beckons, and with inverted torch doth stand
To lead us with a gentle hand
Into the land of the great Departed,
Into the Silent Land!

THE TWO LOCKS OF HAIR.

FROM THE GERMAN OF PFIZER.

A YOUTH, light-hearted and content,
  I wander through the world;
Here, Arab-like, is pitched my tent
  And straight again is furled.

Yet oft I dream, that once a wife
  Close in my heart was locked,
And in the sweet repose of life
  A blessed child I rocked.

I wake! Away that dream, — away!
  Too long did it remain!
So long, that both by night and day
  It ever comes again.

The end lies ever in my thought;
  To a grave so cold and deep
The mother beautiful was brought;
  Then dropt the child asleep.

But now the dream is wholly o'er,
  I bathe mine eyes and see;
And wander through the world once more,
  A youth so light and free.

Two locks, — and they are wondrous fair, —
  Left me that vision mild;
The brown is from the mother's hair,
  The blond is from the child.

And when I see that lock of gold,
  Pale grows the evening-red;
And when the dark lock I behold,
  I wish that I were dead.

THE SINGERS.

GOD sent his Singers upon earth
With songs of sadness and of mirth,
That they might touch the hearts of men,
And bring them back to heaven again.

The first, a youth, with soul of fire,
Held in his hand a golden lyre;
Through groves he wandered, and by streams,
Playing the music of our dreams.

The second, with a bearded face,
Stood singing in the market-place,
And stirred with accents deep and loud
The hearts of all the listening crowd.

A gray, old man, the third and last,
Sang in cathedrals dim and vast,
While the majestic organ rolled
Contrition from its mouths of gold.

And those who heard the Singers three
Disputed which the best might be;
For still their music seemed to start
Discordant echoes in each heart.

But the great Master said, "I see
No best in kind, but in degree;
I gave a various gift to each,
To charm, to strengthen, and to teach.

"These are the three great chords of might,
And he whose ear is tuned aright
Will hear no discord in the three,
But the most perfect harmony."

CHRISTMAS BELLS.

I HEARD the bells on Christmas Day
Their old, familiar carols play,
    And wild and sweet
    The words' repeat
Of peace on earth, good-will to men!

And thought how, as the day had come,
The belfries of all Christendom
    Had rolled along
    The unbroken song
Of peace on earth, good-will to men!

Till, ringing, singing on its way,
The world revolved from night to day,
    A voice, a chime,
    A chant sublime
Of peace on earth, good-will to men!

Then from each black, accursed mouth,
The cannon thundered in the South,
    And with the sound
    The carols drowned
Of peace on earth, good-will to men!

It was as if an earthquake rent
The hearth-stones of a continent,
    And made forlorn
    The households born
Of peace on earth, good-will to men!

And in despair I bowed my head;
"There is no peace on earth," I said;
    "For hate is strong
    And mocks the song
Of peace on earth, good-will to men!"

Then pealed the bells more loud and deep:
" God is not dead; nor doth he sleep!
    The Wrong shall fail,
    The Right prevail,
With peace on earth, good-will to men!"

Cambridge: Electrotyped and Printed by Welch, Bigelow, & Co.